Streaming Analytics

Dr. A. Manju, M. E., Ph. D.,

Made with ❤ on the Notion Press Platform

www.notionpress.com

Streaming Analytics

Introduction to Stream Processing - Batch vs Stream Processing, Examples of stream processing - Map Reduce, Scalability and Fault Tolerance - Applications of stream processing - Stateful Stream Processing - Stream Processing Model - Data Sources, Stream processing pipelines, Sink - Transformations and Aggregation - Window Aggregations - Stateless and stateful processing - Effect of time in stream processing - Lambda Architecture - Kappa Architecture - Examples – Lambda & Kappa Architectures - Streaming vs Batch Algorithms - Applications – Streaming and Batch Algorithms - Use of a Batch-Processing Component in a Streaming Application - Recap – Stream Processing Fundamentals

Introduction to Stream Processing

- Stream processing is the discipline and related set of techniques used to extract information from *unbounded data*.
- Tyler Akidau defines unbounded data as follows: **"A type of dataset that is infinite in size (at least theoretically)".**
- Given that our information systems are built on hardware with finite resources such as memory and storage capacity, they cannot possibly hold unbounded datasets.
- Instead, we observe the data as it is received at the processing system in the form of a flow of events over time. We call this a *stream* of data.
- In contrast, we consider *bounded data* as a dataset of known size. We can count the number of elements in a bounded dataset.

Batch vs Stream Processing

- With *batch processing*, we refer to the computational analysis of bounded datasets. In practical terms, this means that those datasets are available and retrievable as a whole from some form of storage. We know the size of the dataset at the start of the computational process, and the duration of that process is limited in time.
- With *stream processing* we are concerned with the processing of data as it arrives to the system. Given the unbounded nature of data streams, the stream processors need to run constantly for as long as the stream is delivering new data.
- Stream-processing systems apply programming and operational techniques to make possible the processing of potentially infinite data streams with a limited amount of computing resources.

Examples of stream processing

The use of stream processing goes as wild as our capacity to imagine new real-time, innovative applications of data. The following use cases, in which the authors have been involved in one way or another, are only a small sample that we use to illustrate the wide spectrum of application of stream processing:

- ***Device monitoring:*** A small startup rolled out a cloud-based Internet of Things (IoT) device monitor able to collect, process, and store data from up to 10 million devices. Multiple stream processors were deployed to power different parts of the application, from real-time dashboard updates using in-memory stores, to continuous data aggregates, like unique counts and minimum/maximum measurements.
- ***Fault detection:*** A large hardware manufacturer applies a complex stream-processing pipeline to receive device metrics. Using time-series analysis, potential failures are detected and corrective measures are automatically sent back to the device.
- ***Billing modernization****:* A well-established insurance company moved its billing system to a streaming pipeline. Batch exports from its existing mainframe infrastructure are streamed through this system to meet the existing billing processes while allowing new real-time flows from insurance agents to be served by the same logic.
- ***Fleet management****:* A fleet management company installed devices able to report real-time data from the managed vehicles, such as location, motor parameters, and fuel levels, allowing it to enforce rules like geographical limits and analyze driver behavior regarding speed limits.
- ***Media recommendations****:* A national media company deployed a streaming pipeline to ingest new videos, such as news reports, into its recommendation system, making the videos available to its users' personalized suggestions almost as soon as they are ingested into the company's media repository. The company's previous system would take hours to do the same.
- ***Faster loans****:* A bank active in loan services was able to reduce loan approval from hours to seconds by combining several data streams into a streaming application.
- A common thread among those use cases is the need of the business to process the data and create actionable insights in a short period of time from when the data was received. This time is relative to the use case: although *minutes* is a very fast turnaround for a loan approval, a milliseconds response is probably necessary to detect a device failure and issue a corrective action within a given service-level threshold.

Map Reduce, Scalability and Fault Tolerance

MapReduce

MapReduce is a programming API first, and a set of components second, that make programming for a distributed system a relatively easier task than all of its predecessors. Its core tenets are two functions:

Map: The map operation takes as an argument a function to be applied to every element of the collection. The collection's elements are read in a distributed manner through the distributed filesystem, one chunk per executor machine. Then, all of the elements of the collection that reside in the local chunk see the function applied to them, and the executor emits the result of that application, if any.

Reduce: The reduce operation takes two arguments: one is a neutral element, which is what the *reduce* operation would return if passed an empty collection. The other is an aggregation operation, that takes the current value of an aggregate, a new element of the collection, and lumps them into a new aggregate.

Combinations of these two higher-order functions are powerful enough to express every operation that we would want to do on a dataset.

From the programmer's perspective, here are the main advantages of MapReduce:

- It has a simple API.
- It offers very high expressivity.
- It significantly offloads the difficulty of distributing a program from the shoulders of the programmer to those of the library designer. In particular, resilience is built into the model.

Although these characteristics make the model attractive, the main success of Map-Reduce is its ability to sustain growth. As data volumes increase and growing business requirements lead to more information-extraction jobs, the MapReduce model demonstrates two crucial properties:

Scalability

As datasets grow, it is possible to add more resources to the cluster of machines in order to preserve a stable processing performance.

Fault tolerance

The system can sustain and recover from partial failures. All data is replicated. If a data-carrying executor crashes, it is enough to relaunch the task that was running on the crashed executor. Because the master keeps track of that task, that does not pose any particular problem other than rescheduling.

These two characteristics combined result in a system able to constantly sustain workloads in an environment fundamentally unreliable, *properties that we also require for stream processing*.

Applications of stream processing

Applications in which stream processing is most effective include:

- algorithmic trading and stock market surveillance
- computer system and network monitoring
- geofencing and wildlife tracking
- geospatial data processing
- predictive maintenance
- production line monitoring
- smart device applications
- smart patient care
- sports analytics
- supply chain optimization

- surveillance and fraud detection
- and traffic monitoring.

Stateful Stream Processing

Let's imagine that we are counting the votes during a presidential election. The classic

batch approach would be to wait until all votes have been cast and then proceed to count them. Even though this approach produces a correct end result, it would make for very boring news over the day because no (intermediate) results are known until the end of the electoral process.

A more exciting scenario is when we can count the votes per candidate as each vote is

cast. At any moment, we have a partial count by participant that lets us see the current standing as well as the voting trend. We can probably anticipate a result.

To accomplish this scenario, the stream processor needs to keep an internal register of the votes seen so far. To ensure a consistent count, this register must recover from any partial failure. Indeed, we can't ask the citizens to issue their vote again due to a technical failure.

Also, any eventual failure recovery cannot affect the final result. We can't risk declaring

the wrong winning candidate as a side effect of an ill-recovered system. This scenario illustrates the challenges of stateful stream processing running in a distributed environment.

Stateful processing poses additional burdens on the system:

- We need to ensure that the state is preserved over time.
- We require data consistency guarantees, even in the event of partial system failures.

Stream Processing Model

The components of stream processing are:

- Data sources
- Stream-processing pipelines
- Data sinks

Data Sources, Stream processing pipelines, Sink

As we mentioned earlier, Apache Spark, in each of its two streaming systems—Structured Streaming and Spark Streaming—is a programming framework with APIs in the Scala, Java, Python, and R programming languages. It can only operate on data that enters the runtime of programs using this framework, and it ceases to operate on the data as soon as it is being sent to another system.

This is a concept that you are probably already familiar with in the context of data at rest: to operate on data stored as a file of records, we need to read that file into memory where we can manipulate it, and as soon as we have produced an output by computing on this data, we have the ability to write that result to another file. The same principle applies to databases—another example of data at rest.

Similarly, data streams can be made accessible as such, in the streaming framework of Apache Spark using the concept of streaming *data sources*. In the context of stream processing, accessing data from a stream is often referred to as *consuming the stream*.

This abstraction is presented as an interface that allows the implementation of instances aimed to connect to specific systems: Apache Kafka, Flume, Twitter, a TCP socket, and so on.

Likewise, we call the abstraction used to write a data stream outside of Apache Spark's control a *streaming sink*. Many connectors to various specific systems are provided by the Spark project itself as well as by a rich ecosystem of open source and commercial third-party integrations.

In Figure 2-1, we illustrate this concept of sources and sinks in a stream-processing system. Data is consumed from a source by a processing component and the eventual results are produced to a sink.

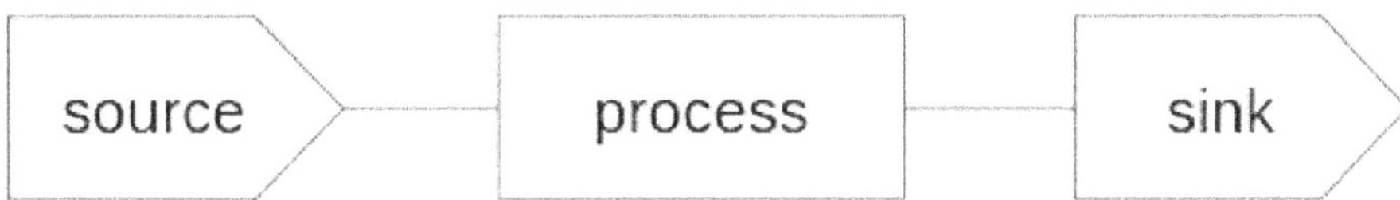

Figure 2-1. Simplified streaming model

The notion of sources and sinks represents the system's boundary. This labeling of system boundaries makes sense given that a distributed framework can have a highly complex footprint among our computing resources. For example, it is possible to connect an Apache Spark cluster to another Apache Spark cluster, or to another distributed system, of which Apache Kafka is a frequent example. In that context, one

framework's sink is the downstream framework's source. This chaining is commonly known as a *pipeline*. The name of sources and sinks is useful to both describe data passing from one system to the next and which point of view we are adopting when speaking about each system independently.

Immutable Streams Defined from One Another

Between sources and sinks lie the programmable constructs of a stream-processing framework. We do not want to get into the details of this subject yet—you will see them appear later in Part II and Part III for Structured Streaming and Spark Stream-ing, respectively. But we can introduce a few notions that will be useful to understand how we express stream processing.

Both stream APIs in Apache Spark take the approach of functional programming: they declare the transformations and aggregations they operate on data streams, assuming that those streams are immutable. As such, for one given stream, it is impossible to mutate one or several of its elements. Instead, we use transformations to express how to process the contents of one stream to obtain a derived data stream.

This makes sure that at any given point in a program, any data stream can be traced to its inputs by a sequence of transformations and operations that are explicitly declared in the program. As a consequence, any particular process in a Spark cluster can reconstitute the content of the data stream using only the program and the input data, making computation unambiguous and reproducible.

Transformations and Aggregation

Spark makes extensive use of *transformations* and *aggregations*. Transformations are computations that express themselves in the same way for every element in the stream. For example, creating a derived stream that doubles every element of its input stream corresponds to a transformation. Aggregations, on the other hand, produce results that depend on many elements and potentially every element of the stream observed until now. For example, collecting the top five largest numbers of an input stream corresponds to an aggregation. Computing the average value of some reading every 10 minutes is also an example of an aggregation.

Another way to designate those notions is to say that transformations have *narrow dependencies* (to produce one element of the output, you need only one of the elements of the input), whereas aggregations have *wide dependencies* (to produce one element of the output you would need to observe many elements of the input stream encountered so far). This distinction is useful. It lets us envision a way to express basic functions that produces results using higher-order functions. Although Spark Streaming and Structured Streaming have distinct ways of representing a data stream, the APIs they operate on are similar in nature. They both present themselves under the form of a series of transformations applied to immutable input streams and produce an output stream, either as a bona fide data stream or as an output

operation (data sink).

Window Aggregations

Stream-processing systems often feed themselves on actions that occur in real time: social media messages, clicks on web pages, ecommerce transactions, financial events, or sensor readings are also frequently encountered examples of such events. Our streaming application often has a centralized view of the logs of several places, whether those are retail locations or simply web servers for a common application.

Even though seeing every transaction individually might not be useful or even practical, we might be interested in seeing the properties of events seen over a recent period of time; for example, the last 15 minutes or the last hour, or maybe even both. Moreover, the very idea of stream processing is that the system is supposed to be long-running, dealing with a continuous stream of data. As these events keep coming in, the older ones usually become less and less relevant to whichever processing you are trying to accomplish.

We find many applications of regular and recurrent time-based aggregations that we call *windows*.

Tumbling Windows

The most natural notion of a window aggregation is that of "a grouping function each x period of time." For instance, "the maximum and minimum ambient temperature each hour" or "the total energy consumption (kW) each 15 minutes" are examples of window aggregations. Notice how the time periods are inherently consecutive and nonoverlapping. We call this grouping of a fixed time period, in which each group follows the previous and does not overlap, *tumbling windows*.

Tumbling windows are the norm when we need to produce aggregates of our data over regular periods of time, with each period independent from previous periods. Figure 2-2 shows a tumbling window of 10 seconds over a stream of elements. This illustration demonstrates the tumbling nature of tumbling windows.

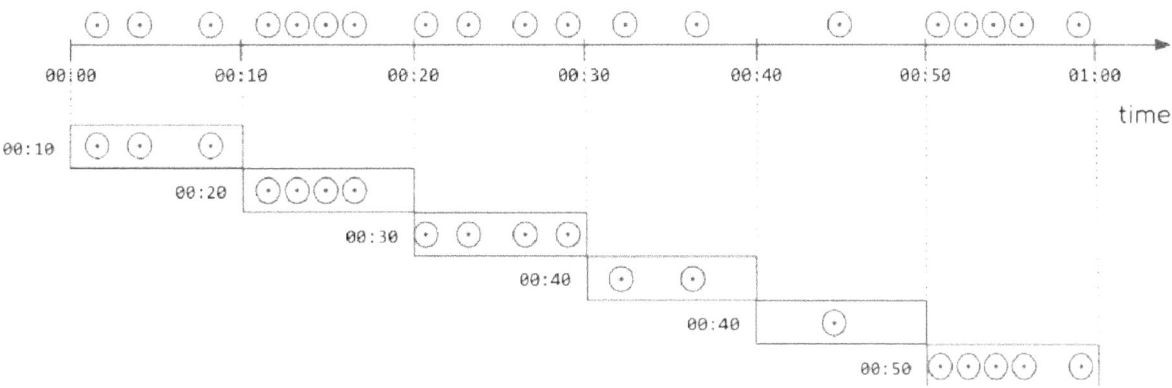

Figure 2-2. Tumbling windows

Sliding Windows

Sliding windows are aggregates over a period of time that are reported at a higher frequency than the aggregation period itself. As such, sliding windows refer to an aggregation with two time specifications: the window length and the reporting frequency. It usually reads like "a grouping function over a time interval *x* reported each *y* fre-you might have noticed already, this combination of a sliding window with the average

function is the most widely known form of a sliding window, commonly known as a *moving average*.

Figure 2-3 shows a sliding window with a window size of 30 seconds and a reporting frequency of 10 seconds. In the illustration, we can observe an important characteristic of *sliding windows*: they are not defined for periods of time smaller than the size of the window. We can see that there are no windows reported for time 00:10 and 00:20.

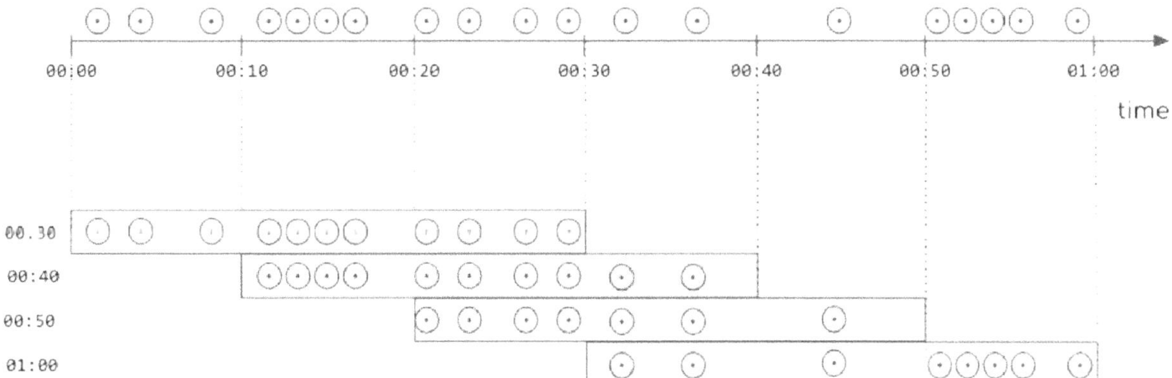

Figure 2-3. Sliding windows

Although you cannot see it in the final illustration, the process of drawing the chart reveals an interesting feature: we can construct and maintain a sliding window by adding the most recent data and removing the expired elements, while keeping all other elements in place.

It's worth noting that tumbling windows are a particular case of sliding windows in which the frequency of reporting is equal to the window size.

Stateless and stateful processing

Now that we have a better notion of the programming model of the streaming systems in Apache Spark, we can look at the nature of the computations that we want to apply on data streams. In our context, data streams are fundamentally long collections of elements, observed over time. In fact, Structured Streaming pushes this logic by considering a data stream as a virtual table of records in which each row corresponds to an element.

Stateful Streams

Whether streams are viewed as a continuously extended collection or as a table, this approach gives us some insight into the kind of computation that we might find interesting. In some cases, the emphasis is put on the continuous and independent processing of elements or groups of elements: those are the cases for which we want to operate on some elements based on a well-known heuristic, such as alert messages coming from a log of events.

This focus is perfectly valid but hardly requires an advanced analytics system such as Apache Spark. More often, we are interested in a real-time reaction to new elements based on an analysis that depends on the whole stream, such as detecting outliers in a collection or computing recent aggregate statistics from event data. For example, it might be interesting to find higher than usual vibration patterns in a stream of airplane engine readings, which requires understanding the regular vibration measurements for the kind of engine we are interested in.

This approach, in which we are simultaneously trying to understand new data in the context of data already seen, often leads us to *stateful stream processing*. Stateful stream processing is the discipline by which we compute something out of the new elements of data observed in our input data stream and refresh internal data that helps us perform this computation.

For example, if we are trying to do anomaly detection, the internal state that we want to update with every new stream element would be a machine learning model, whereas the computation we want to perform is to say whether an input element should be classified as an anomaly or not.

This pattern of computation is supported by a distributed streaming system such as Apache Spark because it can take advantage of a large amount of computing power and is an exciting new way of reacting to real-time data. For example, we could compute the running mean and standard deviation of the elements seen as input numbers and output a message if a new element is further away than five standard deviations

from this mean. This is a simple, but useful, way of marking particular extreme outliers of the distribution of our input elements.1 In this case, the internal state of the stream processor only stores the running mean and standard deviation of our stream —that is, a couple of numbers.

An Example: Local Stateful Computation in Scala

To gain intuition into the concept of statefulness without having to go into the complexity of distributed stream processing, we begin with a simple non distributed stream example in Scala.

The Fibonacci Sequence is classically defined as a stateful stream: it's the sequence starting with 0 and 1, and thereafter composed of the sum of its two previous elements, as shown in Example 2-1.

Example 2-1. A stateful computation of the Fibonacci elements

```
scala> val ints = Stream.from(0)

ints: scala.collection.immutable.Stream[Int] = Stream(0, ?)

scala> val fibs = (ints.scanLeft((0, 1)){ case ((previous, current), index) =>

(current, (previous + current))})

fibs: scala.collection.immutable.Stream[(Int, Int)] = Stream((0,1), ?)
```

```
scala> fibs.take(8).print
(0,1), (1,1), (1,2), (2,3), (3,5), (5,8), (8,13), (13,21), empty
Scala> fibs.map{ case (x, y) => x}.take(8).print
0, 1, 1, 2, 3, 5, 8, 13, empty
```

Stateful stream processing refers to any stream processing that looks to past information to obtain its result. It's necessary to maintain some *state* information in the process of computing the next element of the stream. Here, this is held in the recursive argument of the scanLeft function, in which we can see fibs having a tuple of two elements for each element: the sought result, and the next value. We can apply a simple transformation to the list of tuples fibs to retain only the leftmost element and thus obtain the classical Fibonacci Sequence.

The important point to highlight is that to get the value at the *nth* place, we must process all *n–1* elements, keeping the intermediate (i-1, i) elements as we move along the stream. Would it be possible to define it without referring to its prior values, though, purely statelessly?

A Stateless Definition of the Fibonacci Sequence as a Stream Transformation

To express this computation as a stream, taking as input the integers and outputting the Fibonacci Sequence, we express this as a stream transformation that uses a stateless map function to transform each number to its Fibonacci value. We can see the implementation of this approach in Example 2-2.

Example 2-2. A stateless computation of the Fibonacci elements

```
scala> import scala.math.{pow, sqrt}
import scala.math.{pow, sqrt}
scala> val phi = (sqrt(5)+1) / 2
phi: Double = 1.618033988749895
scala> def fibonacciNumber(x: Int): Int =
((pow(phi,x) - pow(-phi,-x))/sqrt(5)).toInt
fibonacciNumber: (x: Int)Int
scala> val integers = Stream.from(0)
integers: scala.collection.immutable.Stream[Int] = Stream(0, ?)
scala> integers.take(10).print
0, 1, 2, 3, 4, 5, 6, 7, 8, 9, empty
scala> val fibonacciSequence = integers.map(fibonacciNumber)
fibonacciSequence: scala.collection.immutable.Stream[Int] = Stream(0, ?)
scala>fibonacciSequence.take(8).print
0, 1, 1, 2, 3, 5, 8, 13, empty
```

This rather counterintuitive definition uses a stream of integers, starting from the single integer (0), to then define the Fibonacci Sequence as a computation that takes as input an integer *n* received over the stream and returns the *n-th* element of the Fibonacci Sequence as a result. This uses a floating-point number formula known as the *Binet formula* to compute the *n-th* element of the sequence directly, without requiring the previous elements; that is, without requiring knowledge of the state of the stream.

Notice how we take a limited number of elements of this sequence and print them in Scala, as an explicit operation. This is because the computation of elements in our stream is executed lazily, which calls the evaluation of our stream only when required, considering the elements needed to produce them from the last materialization point to the original source.

Stateless or Stateful Streaming

We illustrated the difference between stateful and stateless stream processing with a rather simple case that has a solution using the two approaches. Although the stateful version closely resembles the definition, it requires more computing resources to produce a result: it needs to traverse a stream and keep intermediate values at each step.

The stateless version, although contrived, uses a simpler approach: we use a stateless function to obtain a result. It doesn't matter whether we need the Fibonacci number for 9 or 999999, in both cases the computational cost is roughly of the same order.

We can generalize this idea to stream processing. Stateful processing is more costly in terms of the resources it uses and also introduces concerns in face of failure: what happens if our computation fails halfway through the stream? Although a safe rule of thumb is to choose for the stateless option, if available, many of the interesting questions we can ask over a stream of data are often stateful in nature. For example: how long was the user session on our site? What was the path the taxi used across the city? What is the moving average of the pressure sensor on an industrial machine? Throughout the book, we will see that stateful computations are more general but they carry their own constraints. It's an important aspect of the stream-processing framework to provide facilities to deal with these constraints and free the user to create

the solutions that the business needs dictate.

Effect of time in stream processing

So far, we have considered how there is an advantage in keeping track of intermediary data as we produce results on each element of the data stream because it allows us to analyze each of those elements relative to the data stream that they are part of as long as we keep this intermediary data of a bounded and reasonable size. Now, we want to consider another issue unique to stream processing, which is the operation on timestamped messages.

Computing on Timestamped Events

Elements in a data stream always have a *processing time*. That is, by definition, the time at which the stream-processing system observes a new event from a data source. That time is entirely determined by the processing runtime and completely independent of the content of the stream's element.

However, for most data streams, we also speak of a notion of *event time*, which is the time when the event actually happened. When the capabilities of the system sensing the event allow for it, this time is usually added as part of the message payload in the stream.

Timestamping is an operation that consists of adding a register of time at the moment of the generation of the message, which will become a part of the data stream. It is a ubiquitous practice that is present in both the most humble embedded devices (provided they have a clock) as well as the most complex logs in financial transaction systems.

Timestamps as the Provider of the Notion of Time

The importance of time stamping is that it allows users to reason on their data considering the moment at which it was generated.

For example, if I register my morning jog using a wearable device and I synchronize the device to my phone when I get back home, I would like to see the details of my heart rate and speed as I ran through the forest moments ago, and not see the data as a timeless sequence of values as they are being uploaded to some cloud server. As we can see, timestamps provide the context of time to data.

So, because event logs form a large proportion of the data streams being analyzed today, those timestamps help make sense of what happened to a particular system at a given time. This complete picture is something that is often made more elusive by the fact that transporting the data from the various systems or devices that have created it to the cluster that processes it is an operation prone to different forms of failure in which some events could be delayed, reordered, or lost.

Often, users of a framework such as Apache Spark want to compensate for those hazards without having to compromise on the reactivity of their system. Out of this desire was born a discipline for producing the following:

- Clearly marked correct and reordered results
- Intermediary prospective results

With that classification reflecting the best knowledge that a stream-processing system has of the timestamped events delivered by the data stream and under the proviso that this view could be completed by the late arrival of delayed stream elements. This process constitutes the basis for *event-time processing*.

In Spark, this feature is offered natively only by Structured Streaming. Even though Spark Streaming lacks built-in support for event-time processing, it is a question of development effort and some data consolidation processes to manually implement the same sort of primitives, as you will see in Chapter 22.

Event Time Versus Processing Time

We recognize that there is a timeline in which the events are created and a different one when they are processed:

- ***Event time*** refers to the timeline when the events were originally generated. Typically, a clock available at the generating device places a timestamp in the event itself, meaning that all events from the same source could be chronologically ordered even in the case of transmission delays.
- ***Processing time*** is the time when the event is handled by the stream-processing system. This time is relevant only at the technical or implementation level. For example, it could be used to add a processing timestamp to the results and in that way, differentiate duplicates, as being the same output values with different processing times.

Imagine that we have a series of events produced and processed over time, as illustrated in Figure 2-4.

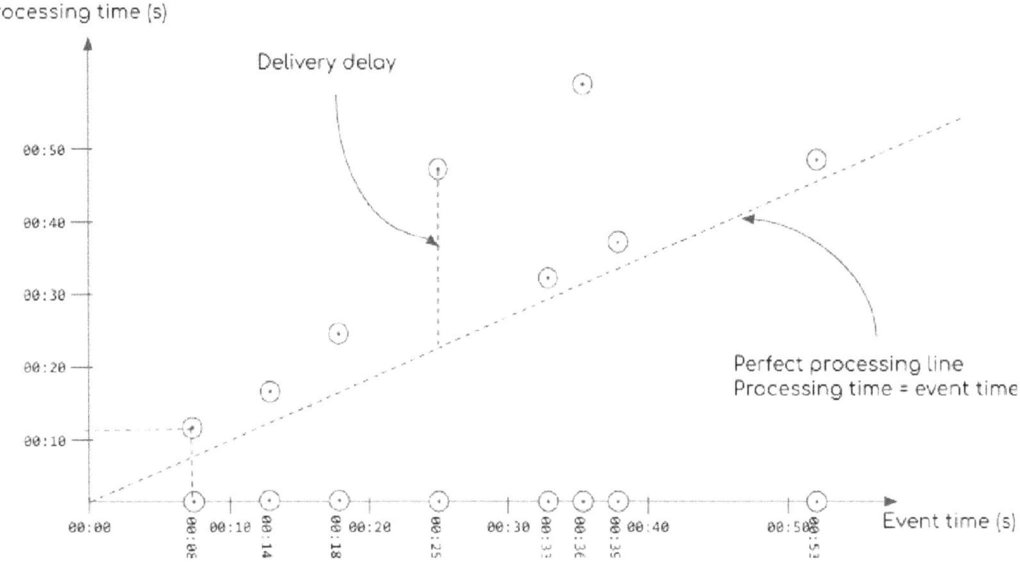

Figure 2-4. Event versus processing time

Let's look at this more closely:

- The x-axis represents the event timeline and the dots on that axis denote the time at which each event was generated.
- The y-axis is the processing time. Each dot on the chart area corresponds to when the corresponding event in the x-axis is processed. For example, the event created at 00:08 (first on the x-axis) is processed at approximately 00:12, the time that corresponds to its mark on the y-axis.
- The diagonal line represents the perfect processing time. In an ideal world, using a network with zero delay, events are processed immediately as they are created. Note that there can be no processing events below that line, because it would mean that events are processed before they are created.
- The vertical distance between the diagonal and the processing time is the *delivery delay*: the time elapsed between the production of the event and its eventual consumption.

With this framework in mind, let's now consider a 10-second window aggregation, as demonstrated in Figure 2-5.

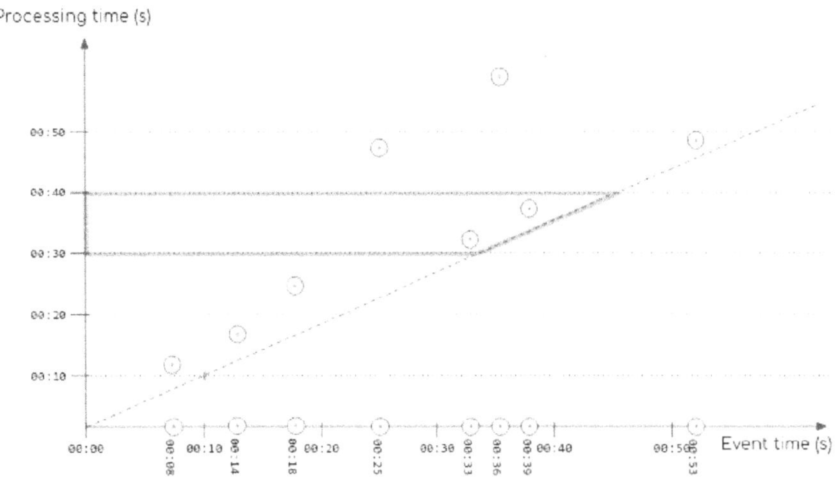

Figure 2-5. Processing-time windows

We start by considering windows defined on processing time:

- The stream processor uses its internal clock to measure 10-second intervals.
- All events that fall in that time interval belong to the window.
- In Figure 2-5, the horizontal lines define the 10-second windows. We have also highlighted the window corresponding to the time interval 00:30-00:40.

It contains two events with event time 00:33 and 00:39. In this window, we can appreciate two important characteristics:

- The window boundaries are well defined, as we can see in the highlighted area. This means that the window has a defined start and end. We know what's in and what's out by the time the window closes.
- Its contents are arbitrary. They are unrelated to when the events were generated. For example, although we would assume that a 00:30-00:40 window would contain the event 00:36, we can see that it has fallen out of the resulting set because it was late.

Let's now consider the same 10-second window defined on event time. For this case, we use the *event creation time* as the window aggregation criteria. Figure 2-6 illustrates how these windows look radically different from the processing-time windows we saw earlier. In this case, the window 00:30-00:40 contains all the events that were *created* in that period of time. We can also see that this window has no natural upper

boundary that defines when the window ends. The event created at 00:36 was late for more than 20 seconds. As a consequence, to report the results of the window 00:30-00:40, we need to wait at least until 01:00. What if an event is dropped by the network and never arrives? How long do we wait? To resolve this problem, we introduce an arbitrary deadline called a *watermark* to deal with the consequences of this open boundary, like lateness, ordering, and deduplication.

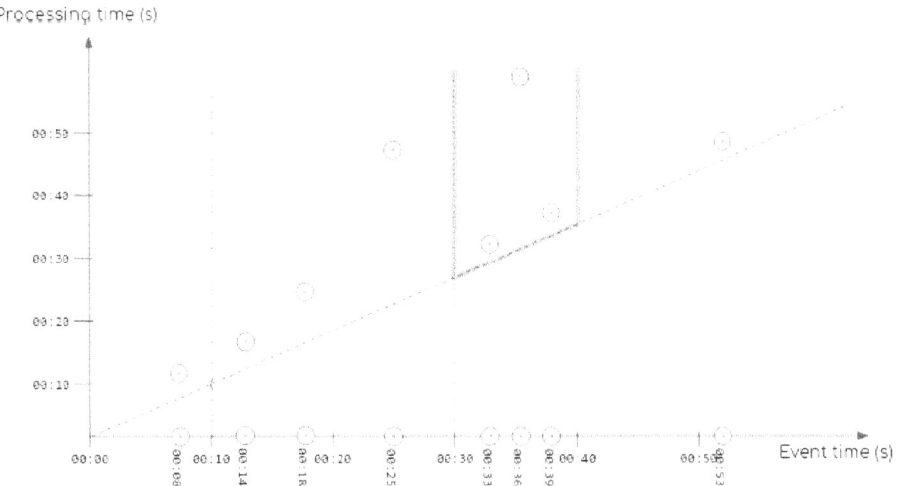

Figure 2-6. Event-time windows

Computing with a Watermark

As we have noticed, stream processing produces periodic results out of the analysis of the events observed in its input. When equipped with the ability to use the timestamp contained in the event messages, the stream processor is able to bucket those messages into two categories based on a notion of a watermark.

The watermark is, at any given moment, *the oldest timestamp that we will accept on the data stream*. Any events that are older than this expectation are not taken into the results of the stream processing. The streaming engine can choose to process them in an alternative way, like report them in a *late arrivals* channel, for example.

However, to account for possibly delayed events, this watermark is usually much larger than the average delay we expect in the delivery of the events. Note also that this watermark is a fluid value that monotonically increases over time,2 sliding a window of delay-tolerance as the time observed in the data-stream progresses.

When we apply this concept of watermark to our event-time diagram, as illustrated in Figure 2-7, we can appreciate that the watermark closes the open boundary left by the definition of event-time window, providing criteria to decide what events belong to the window, and what events are too late to be considered for processing.

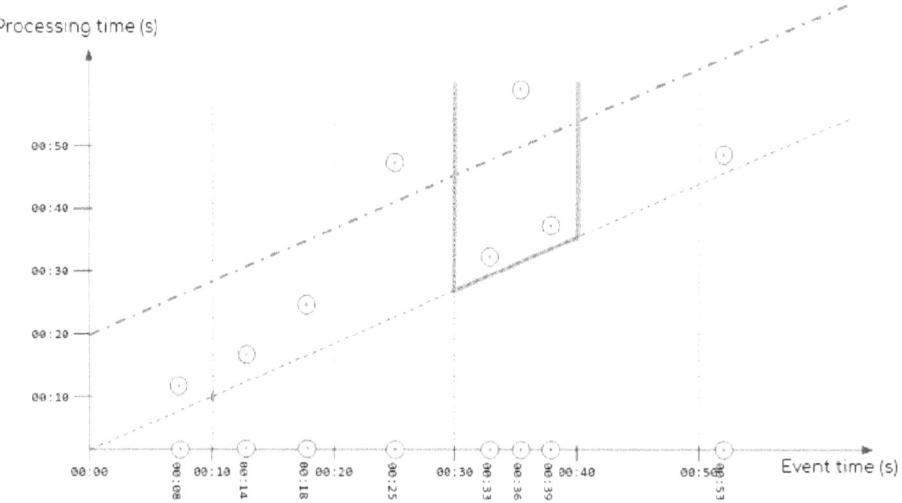

Figure 2-7. Watermark in event time

After this notion of watermark is defined for a stream, the stream processor can operate in one of two modes with relation to that specific stream: either it is producing output relative to events that are all older than the watermark, in which case the output is final because all of those elements have been observed so far, and no further event older than that will ever be considered, or it is producing an output relative to the data that is before the watermark and a new, delayed element newer than the watermark could arrive on the stream at any moment and can change the outcome. In this latter case, we can consider the output as provisional because newer data can still change the final outcome, whereas in the former case, the result is final and no new data will be able to change it.

We examine in detail how to concretely express and operate this sort of computation in Chapter 12.

Note finally that with provisionary results, we are storing intermediate values and in one way or another, we require a method to revise their computation upon the arrival of delayed events. This process requires some amount of memory space. As such, event-time processing is another form of stateful computation and is subject to the same limitation: to handle watermarks, the stream processor needs to store a lot of intermediate data and, as such, consume a significant amount of memory that roughly corresponds to *the length of the watermark × the rate of arrival × message size*. Also, since we need to wait for the watermark to expire to be sure that we have all elements that comprise an interval, stream processes that use a watermark and want to have a unique, final result for each interval, must delay their output for at least the

length of the watermark.

It is left to the users to ensure they choose a watermark suitable for the event-time processing they require and appropriate for the computing resources they have available, as well.

Components of a Data Platform

We can see a data platform as a composition of standard components that are expected to be useful to most stakeholders and specialized systems that serve a purpose specific to the challenges that the business wants to address.Figure 3-1 illustrates the pieces of this puzzle.

Going from the bare-metal level at the bottom of the schema to the actual data processing demanded by a business requirement, you could find the following:

The hardware level

On-premises hardware installations, datacenters, or potentially virtualized in homogeneous cloud solutions (such as the T-shirt size offerings of Amazon, Google, or Microsoft), with a base operating system installed.

The persistence level

On top of that baseline infrastructure, it is often expected that machines offer a shared interface to a persistence solution to store the results of their computation as well as perhaps its input. At this level, you would find distributed storage solu-tions like the Hadoop Distributed File System (HDFS)—among many other distributed storage systems. On the cloud, this persistence layer is provided by a dedicated service such as Amazon Simple Storage Service (Amazon S3) or Google Cloud Storage.

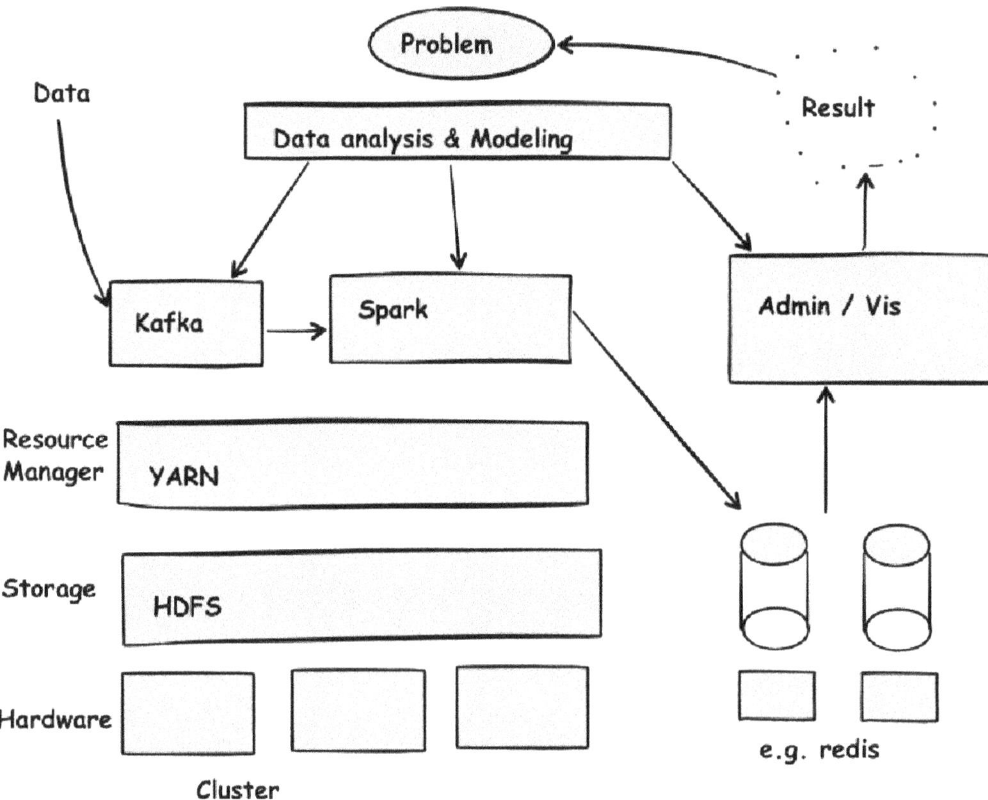

Figure 3-1. The parts of a data platform

The resource manager

After persistence, most cluster architectures offer a single point of negotiation to submit jobs to be executed on the cluster. This is the task of the resource manager, like YARN and Mesos, and the more evolved *schedulers* of the *cloud-native* era, like Kubernetes.

The execution engine

At an even higher level, there is the execution engine, which is tasked with executing the actual computation. Its defining characteristic is that it holds the interface with the programmer's input and describes the data manipulation. Apache Spark, Apache Flink, or MapReduce would be examples of this.

A data ingestion component

Besides the execution engine, you could find a data ingestion server that could be plugged directly into that engine. Indeed, the old practice of reading data from a distributed filesystem is often supplemented or even replaced by another data source that can be queried in real time. The realm of messaging systems or log processing engines such as Apache Kafka is set at this level.

A processed data sink

On the output side of an execution engine, you will frequently find a high-level data sink, which might be either another analytics system (in the case of an execution engine tasked with an *Extract, Transform and Load* [ETL] job), a NoSQL database, or some other service.

A visualization layer

We should note that because the results of data-processing are useful only if they are integrated in a larger framework, those results are often plugged into a visualization. Nowadays, since the data being analyzed evolves quickly, that visualization has moved away from the old static report toward more real-time visual

interfaces, often using some web-based technology.

In this architecture, Spark, as a computing engine, focuses on providing data processing capabilities and relies on having functional interfaces with the other blocks of the picture. In particular, it implements a cluster abstraction layer that lets it interface with YARN, Mesos, and Kubernetes as resource managers, provides connectors to many data sources while new ones are easily added through an easy-to-extend API, and integrates with output data sinks to present results to upstream systems.

Lambda Architecture

The Lambda architecture (Figure 3-2) suggests taking a batch analysis performed on a periodic basis—say, nightly—and to supplement the model thus created with streaming refinements as data comes, until we are able to produce a new version of the batch analysis based on the entire day's data.

It was introduced as such by Nathan Marz in a blog post, "How to beat the CAP Theorem". 1 It proceeds from the idea that we want to emphasize two novel points beyond the precision of the data analysis:

- The historical replay-ability of data analysis is important
- The availability of results proceeding from fresh data is also a very important point

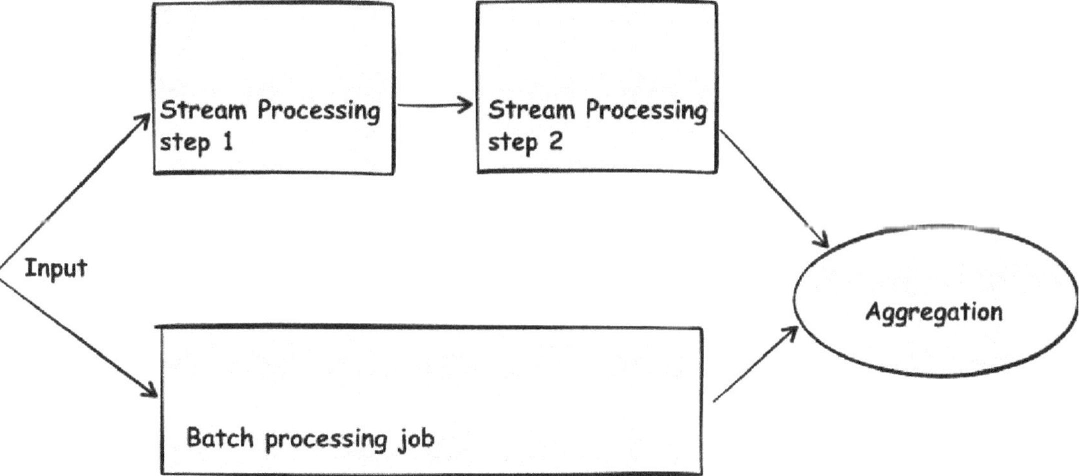

Figure 3-2. The Lambda architecture

This is a useful architecture, but its drawbacks seem obvious, as well: such a setup is complex and requires maintaining two versions of the same code, for the same purpose. Even if Spark helps in letting us reuse most of our code between the batch and streaming versions of our application, the two versions of the application are distinct in life cycles, which might seem complicated.

An alternative view on this problem suggests that it would be enough to keep the ability to feed the same dataset to two versions of a streaming application (the new, improved experiment, and the older, stable workhorse), helping with the maintainability of our solution.

Kappa Architecture

This architecture, as outlined in Figure 3-3, compares two streaming applications and does away with any batching, noting that if reading a batch file is needed, a simple component can replay the contents of this file, record by record, as a streaming data source. This simplicity is still a great benefit, since even the code that consists in feeding data to the two versions of this application can be reused. In this paradigm, called the *Kappa architecture* ([Kreps2014]), there is no deduplication and the mental model is simpler.

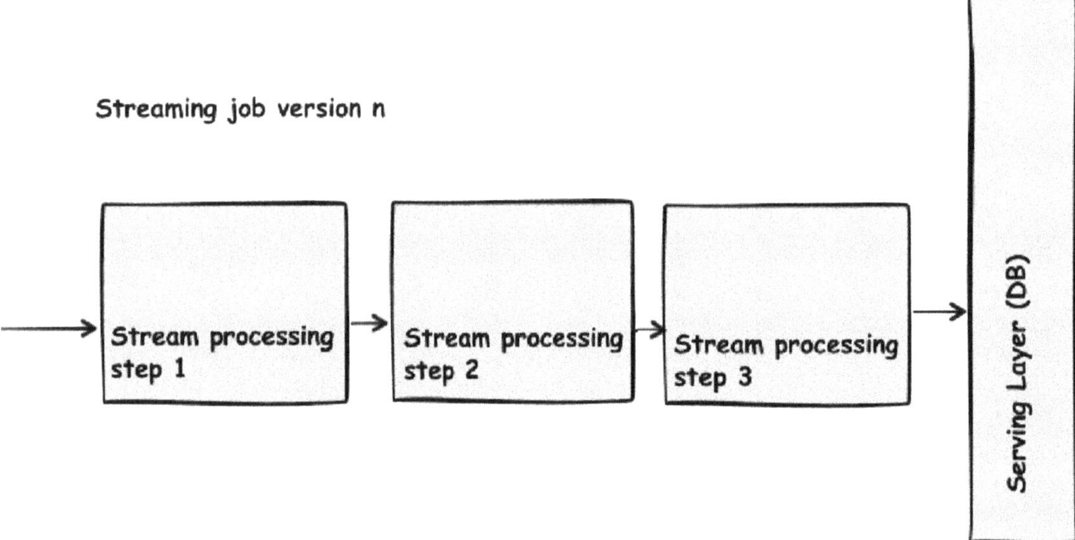

Figure 3-3. The Kappa architecture

This begs the question: is batch computation still relevant? Should we convert our applications to be all streaming, all the time? We think some concepts stemming from the Lambda architecture are still relevant; in fact, they're vitally useful in some cases, although those are not always easy to figure out.

There are some use cases for which it is still useful to go through the effort of implementing a batch version of our analysis and then compare it to our streaming solution.

Streaming vs Batch Algorithms

There are two important considerations that we need to take into account when selecting a general architectural model for our streaming application:

- Streaming algorithms are sometimes completely different in nature
- Streaming algorithms can't be guaranteed to measure well against batch algorithms

Let's explore these thoughts in the next two sections using motivating examples.

Streaming Algorithms Are Sometimes Completely Different in Nature

Sometimes, it is difficult to deduce batch from streaming, or the reverse, and those two classes of algorithms have different characteristics. This means that at first glance we might not be able to reuse code between both approaches, but also, and more important, that relating the performance characteristics of those two modes of processing should be done with high care.

To make things more precise, let's look at an example: the buy or rent problem. In this case, we decide to go skiing. We can buy skis for $500 or rent them for $50. Should we rent or buy?

Our intuitive strategy is to first rent, to see if we like skiing. But suppose we do: in this case, we will eventually realize we will have spent more money than we would have if we had bought the skis in the first place. In the batch version of this computation, we proceed "in hindsight," being given the total number of times we will go skiing in a lifetime. In the streaming, or online version of this problem, we are asked to make a decision (produce an output) on each discrete skiing event, as it happens.

The strategy is fundamentally different. In this case, we can consider the competitive ratio of a streaming algorithm. We run the algorithm on the worst possible input, and then compare its "cost" to the decision that a batch algorithm would have taken, "in hindsight." In our buy-or-rent problem, let's consider the following streaming strategy: we rent until renting makes our total spending as much as buying, in which case we buy.

If we go skiing nine times or fewer, we are optimal, because we spend as much as what we would have in hindsight. The competitive ratio is one. If we go skiing 10 times or more, we pay $450 + $500 = $950. The worst input is to receive 10 "ski trip" decision events, in which case the batch algorithm, in hindsight, would have paid $500. The competitive ratio of this strategy is (2 – 1/10). If we were to choose another algorithm, say "always buy on the first occasion," then the worst possible input is to go skiing only once, which means that the competitive ratio is $500 / $50 = 10.

A better competitive ratio is smaller, whereas a competitive ratio above one shows that the streaming algorithm performs measurably worse on some inputs. It is easy to see that with the worst input condition, the batch algorithm, which proceeds in hindsight with strictly more information, is always expected to perform better (the competitive ratio of any streaming algorithm is greater than one).

Streaming Algorithms Can't Be Guaranteed to Measure Well Against Batch Algorithms

Another example of those unruly cases is the bin-packing problem. In the binpacking problem, an input of a set of objects of different sizes or different weights must be fitted into a number of bins or containers, each of them having a set volume or set capacity in terms of weight or size. The challenge is to find an assignment of objects into bins that minimizes the number of containers used.

In computational complexity theory, the offline ration of that algorithm is known to be *NP-hard*. The simple variant of the problem is the *decision* question: knowing whether that set of objects will fit into a specified number of bins. It is itself NPcomplete, meaning (for our purposes here) computationally very difficult in and of itself.

In practice, this algorithm is used very frequently, from the shipment of actual goods in containers, to the way operating systems match memory allocation requests, to blocks of free memory of various sizes.

There are many variations of these problems, but we want to focus on the distinction between online versions—for which the algorithm has as input a stream of objects— and offline versions—for which the algorithm can examine the entire set of input objects before it even starts the computing process.

The online algorithm processes the items in arbitrary order and then places each item in the first bin that can accommodate it, and if no such bin exists, it opens a new bin and puts the item within that new bin. This greedy approximation algorithm always allows placing the input objects into a set number of bins that is, at worst, suboptimal; meaning we might use more bins than necessary.

A better algorithm, which is still relatively intuitive to understand, is the *first fit decreasing strategy*, which operates by first sorting the items to be inserted in decreasing order of their sizes, and then inserting each item into the first bin in the list with sufficient remaining space. That algorithm was proven in 2007 to be much closer to the optimal algorithm producing the absolute minimum number of bins ([Dosa2007]).

The first fit decreasing strategy, however, relies on the idea that we can first sort the items in decreasing order of sizes before we begin processing them and packing them into bins. Now, attempting to apply such a method in the case of the online bin-packing problem, the situation is completely different in that we are dealing with a stream of elements for which sorting is not possible. Intuitively, it is thus easy to understand that the online bin-packing problem—which by its nature lacks foresight when it operates —is much more difficult than the offline bin-packing problem.

The larger issue presented in this section is that there is no guarantee that a streaming algorithm will perform better than a batch algorithm, because those algorithms must function without foresight. In particular, some online algorithms, including the knapsack problem, have been proven to have an arbitrarily large performance ratio when compared to their offline algorithms.

What this means, to use an analogy, is that we have one worker that receives the data as batch, as if it were all in a *storage room* from the beginning, and the other worker receiving the data in a streaming fashion, as if it were on a *conveyor belt*, then *no matter how clever our streaming worker is, there is always a way to place items on the conveyor belt in such a pathological way that he will finish his task with an arbitrarily worse result than the batch worker*.

The takeaway message from this discussion is twofold:

- Streaming systems are indeed "lighter": their semantics can express a lot of low latency analytics in expressive terms.
- Streaming APIs invite us to implement analytics using streaming or online algorithms in which heuristics are sadly limited, as we've seen earlier.

Use of a Batch-Processing Component in a Streaming Application

Often, if we develop a batch application that runs on a periodic interval into a streaming application, we are provided with batch datasets already—and a batch program representing this periodic analysis, as well. In this evolution use case, as described in the prior chapters, we want to evolve to a streaming application to reap the benefits of a lighter, simpler application that gives faster results.

In a greenfield application, we might also be interested in creating a reference batch dataset: most data engineers don't work on merely solving a problem once, but revisit their solution, and continuously improve it, especially if value or revenue is tied to the performance of their solution. For this purpose, a batch dataset has the advantage of setting a benchmark: after it's collected, it does not change anymore and can be used as a "test set." We can indeed replay a batch dataset to a streaming system to compare its performance to prior iterations or to a known benchmark.

In this context, we identify three levels of interaction between the batch and the stream-processing components, from the least to the most mixed with batch processing:

Code reuse

Often born out of a reference batch implementation, seeks to reemploy as much of it as possible, so as not to duplicate efforts. This is an area in which Spark shines, since it is particularly easy to call functions that transform Resilient Distributed Databases (RDDs) and DataFrames—they share most of the same APIs,

and only the setup of the data input and output is distinct.

Data reuse

Wherein a streaming application feeds itself from a feature or data source prepared, at regular intervals, from a batch processing job. This is a frequent pattern: for example, some international applications must handle time conversions, and a frequent pitfall is that daylight saving rules change on a more frequent basis than expected. In this case, it is good to be thinking of this data as a new dependent source that our streaming application feeds itself off.

Mixed processing

Wherein the application itself is understood to have both a batch and a streaming component during its lifetime. This pattern does happen relatively frequently, out of a will to manage both the precision of insights provided by an application, and as a way to deal with the versioning and the evolution of the application itself. The first two uses are uses of convenience, but the last one introduces a new notion: using a batch dataset as a benchmark. In the next subsections, we see how this affects the architecture of a streaming application.

Recap – Stream Processing Fundamentals

In conclusion, the news of batch processing's demise is overrated: batch processing is still relevant, at least to provide a baseline of performance for a streaming problem. Any responsible engineer should have a good idea of the performance of a batch algorithm operating "in hindsight" on the same input as their streaming application:

- If there is a known competitive ratio for the streaming algorithm at hand, and the resulting performance is acceptable, running just the stream processing might be enough.
- If there is no known competitive ratio between the implemented stream processing and a batch version, running a batch computation on a regular basis is a valuable benchmark to which to hold one's application.

www.ingramcontent.com/pod-product-compliance
Lightning Source LLC
LaVergne TN
LVHW070945160826
845679LV00022B/1911

* 9 7 9 8 8 9 6 7 3 0 6 0 6 *